EMPTY BRANCHES

EMPTY BRANCHES

*A Season of
Zen Teachings*

Bonnie Myotai Treace, Sensei

MILLSTONE PRESS

Dedication

To my mom, who always knew, and it was love.
And to my teachers, who said not to know,
And that, too, was quite likely love.

Table of Contents

Introduction

There is a famous Zen tale in which an angry monk attempts to right a situation he feels has gone horribly wrong by pursuing someone into the mountains and forcibly taking back a teaching robe he's sure should not have been awarded. The robe, symbolizing the authority to be the next teacher in the lineage, had been given at midnight to the rice pounder at the monastery, along with the instructions to lay low for a while to let tensions ease. When the rice pounder, Hui Neng, sees Monk Myo (whom we're told is quite a massive character) approaching, he places the robe on a stone right in front of him. "What is received in faith," he says, "cannot be taken by force." Myo reaches down and tries to pick up the robe, but even using all his strength, he simply cannot lift it. Suddenly his anger, all his self-righteousness, dissolves into tears. "I've come for the teaching," he says, "not for the robe. Please help me."

I'm reminded of the passage by modern philosopher Diogenes Allen: "Mystery withers at the very touch of force. This is a law, a truth that governs us as firmly as any law we have met so far, and as firmly as any that exists in all the permutations of matter and energy. When we treat other people as objects subordinate to our goals, their mystery has no effect on us. The larger mystery into which genuine personal encounter can lead us never becomes open to us."[1]

Empty Branches is an invitation to explore what Allen here refers to as "genuine encounter"—with one another, with one-self, with all things. The stories and verses used are called koans, and the traditional study of them is the process of realizing their truths as directly and intimately as possible. In koan study, abstractions become personal, and the emphasis is always on having a vital, inarguable religious experience.

It is, to say the least, very challenging to not simply carry our agendas forward, as Monk Myo demonstrated and as we all know all so well. There are many grievous issues calling for our brave, intelligent, and diligent response, as well as the future to create with our innovation, imagination, and generosity. Monk Myo's concern was the future of his monastery; for us it is per-haps whether sentient life has another generation or more on planet Earth. Both return to the same crux, the same intense demand: let go in order to receive. *Let go of what?* we ask. *Why can't he lift the robe?* the koan asks. *Whatever you think it is, let go of that, too.*[2]

The last leaf is not the last leaf.

The talks that are now the chapters of *Empty Branches* were given for students both male and female, who traveled some-times long distances, from careers as diverse as adult life might call one to, across racial and economic lines. They assume a con-text of meditation, and I propose a quiet setting for their read-ing. In this, you join in a silent integrity and are part of a com-munion fed by intent. It is simple, and demanding, this work asked of each one of us as we create lives that are more than the chatter and trivia, the fear and anxiety that otherwise fill the mind. Those who gather in the rooms called zendos to sit and study together form immense friendships formed from furthering the deepest longings of the human project: to awaken, to be kind, to not waste the immeasurable gift of life. That friendship extends, of course, beyond all walls, whenever the genuine encounter with the dharma, the teachings, happens without masks, without putting something in between.

An encouragement to those who may be encountering the language of koans for the first time through *Empty Branches:* On the surface, or on first encounter, koans may seem puzzling, or like riddles somehow constructed to trick the mind though clever turns of phrase or obscure references. They are just the opposite. Please hang in: once they become more familiar as a way of unlocking fixed or stuck habits of consciousness, their effectiveness—as well as their elegance and beauty—is revealed. For centuries classic koans have been deemed useful for evoking as well as keeping a record of especially bright and genuine religious experience. A number of Zen teachers today continue the tradition; it is part of how I was trained.

Spring, summer, fall, and winter are the perfect times for our lives to become genuine encounter, whether in kitchen or office, forest or monastery. There is no place you need to go, and everything needed is present. My teacher, John Daido Loori, said this on the matter at hand:

Aside from words and ideas, people don't seem to understand the truth....If you have not as yet seen clearly into this matter, then listen to the sound of the cold wind in the pine trees, look at the autumn mountains of green and gold. When you really see it, it is clearly not like something.[3]

The Broken Tray

The Iron Flute, Case 90

Main Case:
There once was a little hut called
Fei'tien, meaning "rich field,"
where a monk lived for thirty years.
(Fugai: Maybe he did not know how to move.)
He had only one tray made of clay.
(Fugai: Expensive things are not always precious.)
One day a monk, who studied under him, broke that tray
accidentally.
(Fugai: The real treasure appears from the breaking.)
Each day the teacher asked the student to replace it.
(Fugai: Why do you want another?)
Each time the disciple would bring a new one, the teacher
threw it out, saying, "This is not it. Give me back my old one!"
 (Fugai: I would open my hands and laugh.)
(Genro: If I were the disciple, I would say, "Wait until the
sun rises in the west.")
(Fugai: I will search for it before I am born.) [4]

This koan is from one of my favorite collections, *The Iron Flute: 100 Zen Koans*. Translated by Nyogen Senzaki and Ruth Strout McCandless, it was compiled by Master Genro Oryu in the late 1700s. He gathered koans from the Tang (618-907 AD) and Sung (960-1297 AD) dynasty teachings and commented on them. His successor, Fugai, then added a commentary and poem to illuminate each koan's point. Here's the one for the koan of the teacher, the student, and the clay tray:

> *It is broken.*
> (Fugai: The whole tray remains.)
> *Run fast after it.*
> (Fugai: The sword disappears in the water.)
> (Genro: The disciple cannot understand it.)
> (Fugai: It has returned to him already. Call an iron kettle a bell, call the earth heaven…what's wrong?)[5]

It's a wonderful collection in that we are presented with a line of the koan, and then it's as if someone is standing offstage, whispering conspiratorially to us, saying, "Here's the point of what was just said." Although these helpful additions are often as challenging as the original koan, there is a nice sense—if we sit with these whisperings—of having many people working on our behalf for our awakening.

The Iron Flute collection is so named because it takes up koans that deal with doing the impossible. How do you play an iron flute? The holes are closed; it's not a piece of hollowed bamboo where the breath blown through easily transforms into music. How do we do that which can't—but somehow must—be done? How do we reveal what has never been concealed? *The*

Iron Flute koans have an undercurrent of such refreshing vitality that they strike me like cool water cutting through stagnancy; they're designed not to let staleness define our journey. Before we get into this koan, it is important to reflect briefly on how koan study is engaged in formal Zen training.

Because *The Iron Flute* is more modern in its presentation than some of the other collections we use—like *The Blue Cliff Record, The Gateless Gate,* and *The Book of Equanimity*—the language in the koans is a little easier to grapple with. Rather than asking for an intellectual understanding or a philosophical response, koans demand that we experience, realize, and reveal their spirit. In working one-on-one with a teacher, the student who comes in and says, "Well, what this koan means is that all things are one" is rung out by the teacher's bell. That doesn't reach it; that's an explanation. "All things are one" is an idea. If it's not realized, it's not going to transform your way of being, relating to others, or living at ease in the midst of life and death. Showing the Zen teacher that when it rains in Hong Kong it gets wet in Mexico might begin to point at the matter. Even then, though, how could it be shown more personally?

Some of the koan work of Zen is designed to keep spiritual practice from becoming just another variety of self-deceit. Given the proper research materials or time to think, it doesn't take much to talk convincingly about Zen. But koan study is designed to ask "How does it *live*?" If it doesn't live here and it doesn't live now, the koan is not helpful—it's more an intellectual exercise.

In order to study with koans and ensure that they are being taken up deeply, usefully, Zen requires that we work with a teacher. In order to work with a teacher, we need to genuinely become a student with authentic "student mind," enabling training to take place. We often skip over this as we glibly say, "Oh, yes, I want a teacher." It's easy to waste time going through the motions of entering the small room where face-to-face teaching takes place, but to not really be a student in our hearts and minds but rather someone who wants to debate, or to prove something. It's been said and I've found it to be true that once a "student mind" develops, it is inevitable that a teacher will appear in one's life. The student creates the teacher, the teacher creates the student, they create each other.

To meet the teacher in this koan, the student has to enter the hut where the teacher is teaching. To identify with the student is to be in this hut, we don't know where, but we know that this seemingly small place is called "the rich field." In this confined space, the space that seems to have nothing to offer, the place that by all ordinary measures traps us, there is richness. To enter the koan is to identify with this environment, not to separate from Fei'tien. We're asked to consider that perhaps there is more to what confines us than we might immediately assume.

We meet a nameless teacher. I particularly like this koan because the teacher is nameless, and the monk, too, is not given any designation—a dubious honor traditionally reserved for the nuns and traveling laywomen who appear anonymously in the koan collections. Here the nameless student has broken the only tray in the hut, and is being compelled to realize, "What is it that's irreplaceable, unbreakable, and serves continually?"

The teacher demands, "Bring it to me! Show me the tray!" The one who brought about the breaking needs to deal with the brokenness. "It's your job," the teacher implies, nobody else's responsibility. But how can the student produce what doesn't *exist*?

There once was a little hut called Fei'tien, meaning "rich field," where a monk lived for thirty years. Fugai whispers from the sidelines, "Maybe he did not know how to move." Is the teacher stuck? Or is the teacher at the center of the universe, voicing ultimate freedom? It is not clear at this point in the koan, but we need to allow either possibility. Again these comments are delicious, because Fugai is saying, "Don't assume the obvious. Check it out. Maybe the teacher here has nothing to teach." Not knowing how to move could indicate confinement, or it could be the liberty of not knowing, not needing, no other place, no other time, just this place and time filling the universe.

The teacher had only one tray made of clay. Fugai says, "Expensive things are not always precious." Fugai is helping here to identify that the situation of this destitute teacher in his simple hut with its meager supply of serving implements is sufficient; there's more going on than a complaint about the student's clumsiness. The student's situation is in some way the human situation. Whether it is a tray, or a human body, what we have to serve from can seem fragile, and there is only one. What is it that's precious? What is the treasure of the hut?

One day the monk, who studied under the teacher, broke that tray accidentally. Fugai says, "The real treasure begins to appear in the breaking." The body breaks, things change, life ends. Only when impermanence is fully apprehended do we really have the chance to serve, to give without bargaining. So far the monk had only been able to serve what fit on the tray; his teacher wants him to realize and overflow with intimacy. But first, the tray and its limitations—the form and the idea—have to be released.

Each day the teacher asked the student to replace it. Fugai asks, "Do you want another?" Don't think it is somewhere else, some earlier time. Fugai whispered as loudly as he could, but the monk had that cacophony in his brain we all use to drown out the clear song of the iron flute. Don't look elsewhere for it, we're told, don't hesitate or try to remember. Don't call it by your name, or any other name. Just serve.

Each time the disciple brought a new one, the teacher threw it out, saying, "This is not it. Give me back my old one!" Fugai makes two comments here. First he says, "I would just open my hands and laugh!" Then he says, "I will search for it before I am born." The compiler, Master Genro, chimes in, "If I were the disciple, I would say, 'Wait until the sun rises in the West.'" They're all pointing to the same thing: Remaining after all the commentary, after the koans, after the meeting with the teacher is still the matter of this life. The teacher is asking each of us to bring out the tray, to serve not our limitations, but what's whole and unbreakable, our true self. It's easy to identify with all the places we've been hurt and abandoned, but can we identify with the timeless wholeness that weathers every abuse, every condition? If we can't, we may spend this life protecting ourselves and never risk really living. That's why this is such an important koan to realize, over and over.

Another koan, "Keichu Makes Carts" can help clarify how the broken tray koan works. This is a koan from *The Gateless Gate*—or *Mumonkan*—a collection compiled in the early 13th century by the Chinese Zen Master Mumon Ekai. It is the first koan collection students encounter in training. The koan says:

> Master Gettan asked a monk, "Keichu made a hundred carts. If he took off the wheels and removed the axles, what would be vividly apparent?[6]

Keichu was regarded in ancient Chinese mythology as the inventor, the "Adam" of carts. When Keichu is mentioned, we know we're in the realm of primal being, of the original vehicle, the original construction. Keichu's presence is a cue to pay attention not just to the story, but also to the state of consciousness involved. This original cart? He made a hundred of them. Take away the pieces, take away the parts, and what is it that's vividly apparent?

The axle and the wheels are meant to represent all the stuff, all the bits. If we say that what's apparent when the parts are removed is "nothing," that doesn't really reach it. *Nothing* is an idea. Show me *nothing*. The moment you show it, say it, make it, you have turned it into something.

A pile of mechanical bits: wheels, spokes, axles…we might say that is what is made apparent. Still, where do we find ourselves in the koan? This koan could be rephrased as "God made the original person, made a hundred persons, made ten million persons; take away the eyes, the ears, the noses, the shoulders, the fingers, the feet, the guts, the skin—now what is clearly revealed? What is vividly apparent?" *Who are you?*

We grow old, go blind, lose our hearing, can no longer have sex. We've been beautiful, suddenly we get a skin disease; now we're ugly. We've been married, now we're widowed. Some way of defining ourselves changes radically. Who are you? When all the parts and pieces are taken away—all the roles and identities—what's revealed?

Robert Aitken Roshi commented on this using the example of a bicycle. He said:

Zazen is like learning how to ride a bicycle. You have to steer, pump, keep your balance, and watch out for pedestrians and other vehicles—all at once. You are riding a pile of parts with your pile of parts. After you learn to ride, however, what then? You are free of those parts, surely. You are one with the bicycle, and the bicycle keeps its own balance. It steers and pumps itself, and you can enjoy your ride and go anywhere, to the store, to school, to the office, to the beach. You have forgotten sprockets and handlebars. You have forgotten that you have forgotten.[7]

Being one, not separating—the bike rides itself, the dance dances itself. But if we abandon cause and effect in this "forgetting," the koan is not complete. When we carry the tray across the room and drop it, it breaks. If we drive carelessly, we could hurt someone. When one person has ecstatic sex, their partner may still end up bruised and frightened. The limitless body doesn't mean not taking absolute care of *this* one, and absolute care of *that* one. So, how to proceed?

Aitken Roshi said, "Take it off!"

Take off all those parts. Take off all that meat; take away the gristle, the fat, the marrow, the protein, the vitamins, the calcium, the phosphorus, the atoms, the electrons, the neutrons, the protons—and what is crystal clear?[8]

This is hard for us. We don't want to do it. We don't want to let go of our preoccupation with our body and we don't want to let go of the comfort of familiar patterns of thought. To get over the seduction of our own thought is not easy. We're seduced by either self-hatred or self-love. We tell ourselves, "Everything I think and do is inadequate, I'm stupid, I'm too tall, my neck's too long, my eyes are wrong, my hair's too curly or too straight, I don't work as well as I should, I'm not as smart as I should be,

I ought to be doing more, I ought to take better care of myself. Let me define for you why I should not have breathing room on this earth." Or we fall into the other pit: "Let me show you this beautiful thought I've had. Let me explain to you why you should respect me, why you should hear me, why your life won't be complete unless you know all about me, and my stuff, and what I've done and accomplished." Most of us are too busy talking to ourselves to even contemplate what might be vivid and apparent if we could just learn to shut up.

The attachment to the body is similar in that most people tend to swing wildly back and forth between body hate and body love. In explaining our misconception of the body as reality, my teacher Daido Roshi often described a cartoon he wanted to draw in which there's a huge cornucopia of abundant food and other "stuff" we like—apples, bananas, cows, cabbages, music, literature. Everything that we're going to take in is contained in this cornucopia. A sperm and egg come together and form a little being. From the moment of conception, the cornucopia begins to spill into the mouth and eyes and sense organs of the being. The being grows and begins to walk and then to stride and the cornucopia keeps flowing. Very shortly after the flowing in begins, the flowing out begins—the creative outflow of the body—all the piss, poop, songs, poems, etc. The being grows older, becomes bent, gets smaller and smaller. Then finally, "poof" and the being is gone. The question implicit in the animation is, "Who are you?" Are you the cornucopia of goodies? Are you the pile of stuff behind? Where are you? Where do you find yourself?

The koan can be so viscerally discomforting that we'll do whatever we can to avoid confronting it. We feed ourselves with guilt, or we look back at our trail of stuff and admire it, "Look what I've made!" We look back at our constructions and are either disgusted or delighted.

Biologist George Williams critiqued our revering the body at death using a similar argument:

[Religions] *ignore the fact that the "last remains" are just that, the material that happened, at the time of death, to provide the medium of expression for a human life. However long this complex human message was expressed is the duration of time in which the materials were coming and going....The tons of matter that at one time or another were a part of a dead senior citizen are already dispersed throughout the terrestrial ecosystem. A small minority of the dead person's molecules are in orbit around the Earth or sun. Cremation of the matter that happened to be there at the last minute merely hastens an inevitable process.[9]*

When it's all taken apart, who are we?

"Bring me the tray! Reveal it!" The student doesn't just leave the hut and evade the issue, go down to the valley and have a drink. He keeps coming back. "Well, how about this wooden tray?" Or, "I've glued together some of the clay pieces and constructed this other thing." He keeps addressing the matter at hand, though he's looking in the wrong place. The tray is needed, the wholeness of our life is demanded. What excuse is acceptable? "I'm sorry, my mother dropped me, I chipped." "I'm sorry, I can't because I'm too sleepy." "I'm sorry, but I'm not smart enough." "I don't even understand the question, so please excuse me."

The demand is always there; life can't happen without you. Please, present the tray, present your life. The time has come.

There are those who will persist and find the treasure in the hut. In one fascicle of Master Dogen's thirteenth-century Shobogenzo, *Sounds of Valley Streams,* he wrote,

> *It is pitiful that we are living in a treasure mountain and can't see it. If we develop an enlightenment-seeking mind, everything becomes the practice of enlightenment, even if we are in the midst of various worlds of samsara, even if have already wasted much time, it doesn't matter. It is still possible to develop an enlightenment-seeking mind in this lifetime.*[10]

This is like that beautiful story of the pirate who came to the Buddha. The pirate was convinced in his youth by a shaman that the way to become powerful was to create a necklace of the knuckles of the people he killed. So the pirate spent his life murdering and assembling this gruesome necklace of body parts in order to be powerful and invulnerable. Then the pirate met the Buddha and, stripped raw of all his delusions, encountered the horror of what he had created, the brokenness of his tray. He said to the Buddha, "It's too late, I have done what you cannot even imagine." The Buddha replied, "I see what you've done. The world of suffering is immeasurable, the ocean of suffering is vast, but the moment one turns toward the shore of enlightenment, it is revealed."

No matter how far out on the sea of suffering we've sailed, all that is required is to turn toward awakening. It's never too late, but it takes that turning, and no one can do that for us.

Dogen also says, in *Sounds of Valley Streams*, that it's very difficult to find people who wish to study the true Buddhist teaching. Throughout human history, saints and sages have been quite rare. If we try to explain the Buddha-seeking mind, people shut their eyes and ears and run away from the truth. They don't have any introspection, they only have resentment.

It's so perpetually tempting to present our objection, our resentment. It takes most of us a very long time to look within, genuinely, vigorously. I remember I went through a period at Zen Mountain Monastery when it seemed that all I could feel was resentment. I wasn't at peace. I was calm in many ways but I didn't feel at peace. Every dharma talk made me angry. I could barely stay on my little black mat, and everything seemed pretentious and ridiculous. I thought, "Maybe we should all just go have brunch and not pretend that this practice does something." My attitude was black and I was ready to take apart the training, the teacher, the koans, the patriarchal horror of all major world religions, the fool's game of all spiritual practices. One morning it dawned on me that I was actually in an intolerable crisis, and that I had better engage it in crisis mode. I had to quit silently complaining and do something to take care of it, or else this was how I was going to live and die. All I could muster was zazen, and I began to sit like I never had before. Because there was nothing else, because there was an intractability to the loneliness that no one else could touch, because I knew there was really nowhere else to go that would be "better"—zazen, Saturday night until midnight, or all night if that's what it took. It began to turn around, and the practice became my own.

"It is difficult to develop a Buddha-seeking mind, but when you do you should never abandon your initial resolve. From the first, never seek the Buddhist way to receive others' praise."[11] Approval, affirmation, someone saying you're right, you're on the right track, you're doing the right thing—this is how we learn.

The hard point is that none of us will ever really be satisfied with somebody else's standard of practice. We don't have their imperative, their death, their life, but we do have our own. When we trust that, we can't go wrong. Dogen also reminds us not to be swayed by criticism: We know that there are dogs that bark at good people. Don't worry about those barking dogs, and don't resent them, either. It is better to say to them, "You beasts, awaken your Buddha-seeking mind!"

In the poem, Genro wrote: "It is broken…Run fast after it." Fugai commented: "The whole tray remains." To realize this directly is to have eyes like shooting stars, with every action snatching a bolt of lightning. "Run fast after it," he says. Don't be stopped, resolve it, take care of it. Do whatever it takes to serve, to realize, to be yourself.

Fugai says: "The sword disappears in the water." There is no longer any sense of you and it, you and the koan, you and your practice. Completely immersed in the way, the way becomes you. The resistance gone, the sharp edges move through the body of water as needed.

Genro says: "The disciple can't understand it." Fugai says: "It's returned to him already, Still, he goes looking for it, outside himself. Call an iron kettle a bell." There is no substitute. If it doesn't ring through you from the top of your head to the tips of your toes, it's not the bell. Fugai says: "You can call the earth heaven…what's wrong?"[12]

It's possible to conclude with something more positive than "I'm a wounded healer, I'll serve from my brokenness." That's still an idea. We can bury ourselves in shit and call it Heaven, but ultimately the situation stinks. It doesn't serve. More than just selling ourselves another story, we can realize the truth of this koan and bring it to life. That unnamed teacher who calls, "Bring me the tray!" each day is still calling. The koan is never over; it is only now, and now makes for an incredibly rich field. Everything we need is in the "small hut" of this moment; everything depends on whether we come forward with the original tray.

Memorial Poem for Marc Poirier

Autumn leaves
too soon under
ancient ash and linden.
Its garden hidden
behind house walls
a blur, broken petals, breeze.
But, man, how you sang.
How it shook the sky.
Be true: that was all of it.
Take it home.
Take it all the way home.

Aiiyyee…

There may be
no beginning nor end
Still, it is hard
not to want
one more season…

Dogen Cubed

You may be familiar with the phenomena known as the Necker cube: a way of drawing two squares and connecting the corners with lines so that the mind recognizes the configuration as a representation of a cube. As we engage it visually, there is a moment where we see the surface and depth one way, and then it seems to shift. What had been the foreground drops back, becoming the depth. The longer we look at the drawing, the more disturbing the fluctuation becomes. The only way to hold the cube in perspective is to pay attention to one particular corner of the drawing, which requires a physical tension, a concentration. If we do that for a moment, we gain a sense of stability within our consciousness, but it's difficult to maintain. Focusing on a Necker cube strikes me as similar to studying the teachings of Zen Master Dogen, who often forces an oscillation of consciousness between what we at first may think is obvious and superficial and what feels deeper and more sacred. As soon as our understanding begins to rest in any interpretation, the top sinks, the bottom rises, sacred becomes mundane, mundane becomes sacred.

Dogen's teachings reach into the heart of that frustration, asking how a path—something that is by definition partial in that it "leads *to*"—can also reveal completeness, oneness, and the wholeness of mind. This is the natural koan of consciousness. We are one, whole and complete without reason for fear, distance, or lack. Yet in the midst of that, how do we account for the recurrent sense of loneliness that sometimes touches each of us, or for the penetrating fear of being harmed, or dying? There is work to be done, a home ground to be found, and yet we sense that whatever can be produced or arrived at is... not quite it.

There are some wonderfully dynamic passages in Dogen's *Sounds of Valley Streams, Forms of Mountains,* the twenty-fifth book of his Shobogenzo, in which he takes up the paradoxes of the spiritual path in just the way we look at a Necker cube. When we go seeking wholeness, the very act of seeking breaks us away from what we pursue. Dogen wrote:

You will scale mountains and sail seas searching for a true teacher and seeking the Way of reality. When you sincerely seek a guide, spiritual benefactors and teachers of the Way descend from heaven and gush out of the earth. At the place where you contact them, they evoke expressions of sentient beings and insentient beings that you hear with the body and hear with the mind. If you listen with your ears, it is the household's everyday tea and meals. But when the eye hears sounds, it is the unconditioned. When you see Buddhas, you see Buddhas in yourself and Buddhas in others, large Buddhas and small Buddhas. Don't be surprised or frightened by large Buddhas, don't feel put off by small Buddhas.[13]

Part of what is so powerful about this particular passage is its confidence in the completion of the path. It is a reminder that because the path is already complete, each of us is able to realize it. Dogen's words come to us in our doubt and offer this loving confidence. *You will complete it. You and It are not apart, therefore you will scale mountains, you will take whatever journey is yours, encounter whatever difficulty is necessary. You will not be diverted; you will not ever be parted from the True Way.*[14] The challenge of that beginning is to recognize where Dogen stands when he offers this compassionate encouragement. What is our relationship with his position, and the basic confidence he speaks out of?

Once, when I was watching the kids in the playground of the local elementary school, it became clear to me how many of us lose that deep sense of ourselves. I love to spend time around groups of children—it's like watching the skittering bugs on top of pond water or dogs hanging out in the city dog run. There's this endless coming together and falling apart—a mini-community of like-mindedness. The fourth-grade girls were practicing for track and had set up five low hurdles. One by one they hurled themselves at these barriers. It was great, like skipping stones flying and landing again and again. They bounced off the ground over a barrier, and over another and another. I watched as one scraggly-haired little girl came up for her turn. She took off full-tilt, making the first barrier, the second, the third, and the fourth. But on the fifth, her heel caught, the hurdle tumbled, and there was a moment of "Oh, no!" as she fell, and all her forward motion came to a standstill.

She collected herself, got up, and ran to the back of the line, but it was obvious that the "Oh, no" of the fifth hurdle was encircling her like a dark cape. As the girls went through one more round, her whole presence became darker and darker. Finally, it was her turn again. She took off, hair flying, running toward the first barrier. Right at the moment when she should have begun her jump, she did this weird little embarrassed dance and then scuttled off, placing herself at the back of the line again. More than anything in the world, I wanted her to have the perfect coach at that moment, one who would shake her up, encourage her to go back out there, and get her to take off the "cape." It wouldn't matter if she did one barrier, or five, or five thousand, if she knocked all five down and started her own special dance of destruction. It wouldn't matter if she started a revolution in the school, saying, "We will no longer spend our time jumping over little white fences; we have better things to do!" *Just go!* Someone needed to help her know it was important to go forward—a coach who would recognize whether what was needed was a hug or a firm shout. I wanted that for her, because finding those guides is such a tremendous treasure.

In an interview in *Writers at Work* in 1988, E.L. Doctorow said , that writing is "like driving a car at night. You never see further than your headlights, but you can make the whole trip that way."[15] He knew—like Dogen in his way—that it's critical that we get into the car, that we turn on the ignition and go. The way will find us as soon as we're on the road.

A student asked Zen Master Sozan, "The teachings say that everyone who falls down on the ground must stand up again by relying on the ground. What is the meaning of 'to fall down'?" Sozan said, "If you affirm the situation, that is the answer." The student said, "What is the meaning of standing up?" Sozan said, "Just stand up!"

This is more than just cheerleading. What is it to fall down? So often, like that little girl who walked away wrapped in darkness, we decide "falling down" is a mistake. We think hitting the ground, knocking over the barrier is a mistake, but the ground we hit, the failure we experience is *not* a mistake. The world is endlessly mysterious; experience is profound to a degree that will always surprise us. It is never a mistake. To foster even a meager appreciation of that (and when we're in the midst of a fall, meager is pretty big) is to begin to practice, to raise bodhicitta, the Bodhi mind, our innate pure mind that can end all suffering. It is the decision to stop complaining and to start paying attention. Contained in the fall is exactly what we need to stand. Everything we need is available, but we have to invite it. What is it to invite reality?

Dogen asks us: *Without arising wholehearted will for the Buddha way, how can anyone succeed in this most important task of cutting the endless round of birth and death?*[16] Again, the wholeheartedness of the will is confidence in the completion of the path, in the effort of the Way. The wholeness is the effort, and the effort is the wholeness. Dogen realizes that this is not a conflict: discipline and delight are not two things, coming home and being home are not two things. He and all the teachers, coaches, and mentors on our side constantly work for us, pull us back into the Way with this reminder. Those who have this drive—even if they have little knowledge or are of inferior capacity, even if they are stupid or evil—will, without fail, gain enlightenment. At many Buddhist temples this is made visual by a sword planted in rock at the entrance. The key is not the removal of the sword from the rock, but the very fact of its presence: impossible, yet present; cannot be, yet exists.

Dogen teaches us that "to arouse such a mind, one must be deeply aware of the impermanence of the world. This realization is not achieved by some temporary method of contemplation."[17]

To me, this is one of the most important teachings of Master Dogen. He was a great codifier and organizer of training systems, yet here he seems to be clarifying that what is key isn't the system itself. The truth is not some method you can take up. You stand alone, raw and dying under heaven and earth. What do you make of it?

Do not wait, Dogen says, *for the teachings from others, the words of the scriptures, and for the principles of enlightenment. We are born in the morning and die in the evening; the man we saw yesterday is no longer with us today.*[18] These are facts we see with our own eyes and hear with our own ears. But do we really notice our impermanence? Do we let it touch us in the midst of being bored, or tired, or incapable? We were born this morning, we will die this evening: how will we give life to this moment?

To realize our potential, Dogen says, we only need arouse and invite that reality, notice and appreciate it: *Even though we live to be seventy or eighty, we die in accordance with the inevitability of death. How will we ever come to terms with the worries, joys, intimacies, and conflicts that concern us in this life? With faith in the Way, seek the true happiness of nirvana.*[19]

If we're satisfied with life on the sidelines, watching others leap over the barriers, content with being half-assed—we never live. What if, as the Jack Nicholson movie suggested, this is as good as it gets? If, on the other hand, we come to terms with our worries by realizing who we are, and by taking up our real work, today, *just as we are*—that is unstoppable life. It is the life we are called to and supported in. It is the life of right now; no excuses, no waiting for a better koan, a different configuration. Practicing the shallows wholeheartedly, we may discover the ocean.

The true happiness of nirvana that isn't conditional to good fortune is our birthright. How can those who are old, or have passed the halfway point in their lives relax in their studies when there is no way of telling how many years are left? Again, Master Dogen rings that bell. One of the difficulties with awareness of impermanence as a wake-up bell is that it creates the same tension required to visually fix a Necker cube in one perspective or another. We know that birth and death are not the whole picture. We are subtly aware of the unborn and the undying. That flexibility of perspective can create either tension or peace, depending on how we take up the moment. The moment itself is both complete and fleeting. We have to keep going. We can't stick with what we knew yesterday, or how we felt this morning: now it stands, now it falls. Everything depends on it. Dogen taught: *It descends from heaven and gushes from the earth.*

Master Dogen called the sangha of Master Yakusan "Daisorin," which means "a great Buddhist temple," or place of true practice. He called it this even though the members of the order numbered no more than ten, and they often had no money to buy oil for the lamps. One night, Master Yakusan had no light. He preached to his disciples, "I have something to say. When an excellent ox is about to bear a calf, I will say it to you." An "excellent ox" is a Zen student on the verge of awakening, someone on the verge of giving birth to the Way. It's also impossible—oxen can't give birth to anything. So, when the impossible happens, he taunted them, we'll talk. At this, a priest walked forward and said, "An excellent ox has given birth to a calf, so master, why don't you speak?" The calf is born. The goose is out of the bottle. It's complete. Hell has frozen over. The truth the monk is presenting is the truth that enlightenment has never been hidden; there is nothing to wait for, nothing lacking. The master said,

"Fetch a light and come here." Here they are in the darkness. There was no oil. Fetch a light, he said, and show me this miraculous birth, this capacity for the darkness of the absolute to give birth to the Way. Make a path to right where you are. Serve all beings. Not later, not with pretty words—right now. He pressed the priest to show him the reality itself. The priest returned to the group of disciples. Did he bring the light, or not? Yakusan encouraged him not to be satisfied with cleverness. Because a koan is not abstract, we are all challenged as well. Did Yakusan say what he had to say, or is there more to be revealed? The path these two are on is endless—somehow, I don't think they will let it fatigue them.

Ceaseless practice, the endless path, can ignite our lives. Daido Roshi often spoke of the fairytale of the ugly duckling's realization of its true nature—of its perfection as a swan and the peace inherent in that moment; the duckling is no longer in doubt about its place, its life, its funky honk. I wonder about the morning after. The swan has been enlightened, and yet it has a lifetime of feeling stupid, out of it, and not good enough that will require dealing with. It developed its muscles in a duck-like fashion rather than a swan-like fashion, and there will probably arise a moment when it looks at the other swans and says, "Her neck is so much more elegantly turned than mine. Although I'm a swan, she is somehow more swan than I." Or a moment when because of those waddle years, the swan realizes that it can outswim the other swans, and even if that swimming is in service of all fowl, there is a subtle arising of ego, of superiority. Only the ugly duck who ceaselessly practices will see that separation, see the perfection of its practice and life, realize it and keep swimming.

Dogen says: *At this place where you contact the true teachers, they evoke expressions from sentient beings and insentient beings so that you hear with the body and hear with the mind. If you listen with your ear it is the household's everyday tea and meals. When the eye hears sounds, this is the unconditioned.*[20]

If the attention we begin with is just this attention of "everyday tea and meals," fine, we start there. Hear with the ear, but don't turn away. Let it deepen, let the bottom rise to the surface, the background to the foreground. The only way to do that is to not turn away. When we stay with that attention, often whatever we thought was the truth begins to open up, to change, transforming us as it transforms. It's like that scene in the movie about Picasso's life when he's riding on a train and someone sits down next to him. Recognizing who he is, the person asks, "Why don't you paint people the way they really are?" Picasso asks, "What do you mean by 'the way they really are'?" The man eagerly pulls out his wallet and shows Picasso a picture of his wife and says, "This is my wife." Picasso responds, "She looks rather small and flat, don't you think?"

When we are unable to commit because we feel there's a better reality around the bend, we wear ourselves out with the journey. It's all ordinary tea and meals, the fare of daily life and practice, the way of fatigue and complaint. But there is another way. We need only to look again at the oscillating cube, the path and the perfection. In that moment the unstoppable, unbounded energy of sacred activity manifests as this life. Our work consists of simply not looking away.

Adirondack Memorial for Daido Roshi

Lake lapping on dock
Everything he needed fit
Into this canoe

The Unspoken Thing

During the weeks after September 11, 2001, I worked with families as they made memorial visits to Ground Zero. The trips began at the Family Assistance Center in Manhattan, where death certificates were issued and other support services arranged. The center was very big and very busy. From there we boarded a ferry to Ground Zero, the still-smoldering World Trade Center site. There were gunboats everywhere we looked in New York Harbor, and on the boat there was significant security. The wind blew brisk and the water incongruously glistened. On the way, the clergy and mental health workers made what connections they could with the families, offering support or space as needed. When we arrived at the site, we walked up into the memorial area, and basically bore witness.

The metaphor of the site visit was so bare it stripped words down to the simplest speech, the most primary matter. From the world of business at the dock, where everyone was involved in taking care of the paperwork and assembling the resources to survive, we made a raw journey down the river to the charnel grounds. Arriving, all business stood still. Conversation withered.

It smelled very bad there. The buildings that remained standing seemed normal until you looked up and saw how parts near the top or on a side had been torn off. Their jagged edges seemed to be gesturing as if caught in mute pain, like a woman raped, walking away, trying to look ordinary but with her dress torn, bruises rising. The clergy's work was to attend to the families, so I turned my attention from the site to them, and we spent fifteen or twenty minutes being there together, offering flowers at the temporary memorial alcove. When it was time for them to take the next step, the next breath, we took it together.

Placing a hand on the small of a crying woman's back, it felt like her bones dissolved for a moment, then she leaned in, slowly her bones reformed. I remembered the words of twelfth-century Zen Master Hongzhi: *Only silence is the supreme speech. Only illumination the universal response.*[21] When someone was ready for talk, talk came. Since there was so obviously nothing to do that was adequate to the pain, all that seemed possible was love. We just were that, loving those whose bodies were buried there, each other, the moments when eyes met, hands touched. Some constructed a palpable, fragile crust of solitude around themselves, and though we kept an eye out to make sure they were safe, there was a tacit agreement to let them be alone. (Actually, some of the clergy had to be reminded to let folks alone. At one morning meeting we were told, "Someone overheard a family member saying to another, 'Whatever you do, don't cry, or the clergy will come…' So those who don't know when to back off, learn!") The flowers and teddy bears left by mourners were piled high and thick, kid-scrawled notes on some, photos and poems on others.

As we boarded the ferry to return to the family assistance center, there was a subtle shift in the energy, a change in how the grief was happening. During each return trip, the work of being clergy changed to protecting the spiritual process of each person on board.

Kirsten Bakis, in her brilliant novel *Lives of the Monster Dogs*, wrote, "In the space between desire and despair, between holding and letting go, between clinging and release, and between my desire for you and my desire for your happiness, which things cannot exist together, and yet which could not exist separately… Can you see this? In this space is the unspoken thing, the thing that lives."[22] In the work on this boat, like the work with my Zen students, I found that there was a chance to enter that space. As each of us in the sangha find our way through practicing with grief and the other emotions that emerge, it can help to acknowledge and protect that space. I'm talking about the space that doesn't know, doesn't know why, doesn't know what's next. It doesn't know bad or good. It is that space relieved of needing something other than what is: relieved of desire. It is the moment that is relieved of the sad predictions: relieved of despair. It just is, and in that is the only real refuge. Call it "the moment," yet even that doesn't clearly indicate its strength and spaciousness. Unspoken, unnamable. Without securing ourselves in any way, we are intimate. Being at zero, if you will. Walking from zero.

More than ever, in the weeks after 9/11 I came to appreciate the practice of zazen, the authenticity of its refuge among so many basically false "answers" to the anxiety of being. We've had so much that is inauthentic sold to us, and we sell false hope to one another. We may take temporary refuge in probability: it is statistically unlikely that any individual one of us will be tremendously harmed or killed on a given day. We take temporary refuge in power: we have one of the best-funded, best-trained militaries in the world, and economic influence that is unparalleled in its capacity to put pressure where pressure is deemed needed. We take refuge in medicine: if we are exposed to a chemical or biological agent, it is likely that we will get treatment, and the survival rates are in our favor.

These false refuges fail to reach the bottom of our anxiety, because they don't sufficiently deal with the issue. The issue, in one sense, is that although we can do our best to secure an outcome, we can't *guarantee* it. We can't know that we will live, or that those we love will live. We can't know whether we will be well, or whether others will be well. We can medicate ourselves with probabilities, but we can't cure the disease that way. *We can't know.* The only real refuge, the only cure, is "the unspoken thing." Being this moment. Just that. Zazen is the training to realize this, and Zen practice is the life it creates. It is the ability to take the step that is here. The bell rings, we bow and practice.

Why go consciously, literally, to where death is? Why end each night of practice with the Evening Gatha?

> Let me respectfully remind you,
> Life and death are of supreme importance.
> Time swiftly passes by and opportunity is lost.
> Each of us should strive to awaken…
> …awaken.
> Take heed. Do not squander your life.

The clear and raw symbolic movement, the intrinsic liturgy of zazen should really be appreciated. The journey of it, to the ground of being, is the visit to Ground Zero every moment. The bell rings to signal walking meditation, the boat comes into the dock and we unload at the pier. How will we step forward from ourselves? This is the loneliest and most important work of any of our lives, in that no one can really tell us anything but that it is possible. To do it is to live it, and to live it may require feeling things that we'd like to avoid. We can't predict; we can only practice.

Someone asked, "But when I don't know who I am, where I'm going, what it means, how can I trust enough to breathe, to move one foot forward and begin?" This is so much the heart of any religious inquiry, any awakened human heart. It's a delicate journey, and it's difficult to do honestly and in a way that doesn't add anything extra. In order to do this work, it is helpful to agree ahead of time to forgive ourselves and one another, and to be forgiven for the missteps that we'll inevitably make. We'll discern when our clarity fails, when we become in any way compulsively protective of that which can't be protected. We'll err, our words will go tin, the connection will grow cloudy, and the only thing that will save us is the capacity to take the next breath together, to not let it break the process that we're in the midst of.

No one can skip grief. One of the problems religious institutions are prone to, according to grief studies, is that when they experience a loss within their congregation, they turn so quickly to the teachings of their tradition to secure themselves emotionally that they may lose the wisdom and honesty of what they've experienced together. A pastoral care instructor once told the story of a church where someone came in the back door during a service and shot the minister in the head, killing him. After burying the minister, the congregation rallied together and became very fervent in their prayer and song, committed to not being brought down in any way by this tragedy. By the time a replacement minister was assigned and began working with them, they had such repressed fear and anger that it took enormous effort to open them up and let them do what they really needed to do: *grieve*. They were singing loud and steady, but they were fighting among themselves about all sorts of trivial things. They needed to trust that their tears and their doubts, their anxiety and their anger, could all be part of their prayer. That way it would be honest and real, and they could love one another and their tradition more fully.

As Zen students individually and as a community, we have our own variations on this desire to skip the grief. We need to be careful not to judge each other's practice, particularly now. We can respect the wholeness of our practice by letting the tears come when it is their time to come, and the fear, and the anger, and the love. Nothing breaks real practice if we let everything be practiced. Please take care of your own practice and your community's by being honest, and respecting one another.

In *Lives of the Monster Dogs*, there is a point at which the dogs, who have been through a journey full of horror and yet found ways to be honorable, are dying:

We are all burning, we are all murdered, anyone who lives is consuming himself, rushing avidly toward the sword, the disease, the accident, toward the day on which his life will end. One is not murdered just at the moment when the blade pierces him, and he knows he will die. For we always know that we are going to die; it is only a question of time, and however long it will take, it is always a certainty, as certain as if we had already received the fatal wound.

So we burn...but we must burn joyfully, and give off light. Our little glowing hearts grow smaller every minute, and with them, the length of time we have left on this earth, and yet we must go on, for there is nothing else to do.[23]

This passage is followed by a reflection on how the speaker has loved and been loved, and the ways in which that is ineffably shown: the contact of the hand on the arm, the eye meeting the eye.

Those are the things that remain unsaid, the little sparks. They cannot exist on their own; they must cling to something else, for they are nothing in themselves; they only make up the spaces in between those things that can be perceived.

You, inside your nets of blood and nerves, are always surrounded by these empty spaces. They are sparks of light. The earth is full of them, and so is heaven, full of little sparks.[24]

Between perceptions…what is that? Of course, these words are not from some ancient Zen tome, and perhaps they are not trustworthy as teaching from your point of view. But don't these words reflect aptly the practice that is not knowing, that enables us to place our practice in the midst of suffering, freely, and to experience our burning as illumination, not despair?

I often wake in the morning in intense pain. My nerves and muscles get inflamed easily. I work with what can be worked with, having studied healing and medicine for many years, and can often ease things through chi kung, stretching, diet, and warm water. Sometimes, though, nothing relieves the hurting, and there may be times when my coordination and other capacities are less available. Practicing "just letting that be" has been my greatest teacher. The desire to have it be otherwise can be strong if I let it get going, and creates more pain. The despair over what it means or indicates about my future can get fierce if I let it have much energy. To place my practice in the "space between" and live there saves my life. It is life. To walk from there is to just walk, even if sometimes that walk is a bit gimpy. The confidence I have about the truth of practice comes from having studied with this "teacher" for almost thirty years. Practice is the only refuge. All the rest is just aspirin, and aspirin fades after a couple of hours, and never really reaches the pain anyway.

Everyone I've met in practice has some natural "teacher" like this, whether it's a crummy childhood, a physical illness, or intractable depression. Many have much more difficult teachers than I, and some people ignore their teacher altogether for long years. But our teachers fuel our spiritual fire, burning away the illusions that separate us, warming our hearts up. Eventually something brings us to zero. There's no way to guarantee safety, or good health, or world peace: there is, however, practice—which is refuge, and wholeness, and this great earth itself. That's enough. Even when we're hurting, that's enough. And sometimes it's actually wonderful. The tight focus on and sense of the significance of our personal pain slowly opens up a bit, and given time, anything can happen. Have you seen a meteor shower? Hundreds of stars falling? Hundreds. Brief, bright blazes in the black morning. We can call it a "meteor shower," but that barely satisfies. From an old poem I wrote: *Up until that moment, I hadn't realized I had lived my life for that moment.*

Hongzhi taught:

Responding without falling into achievement, speaking without involving listeners,

The ten thousand forms majestically glisten and expound the dharma…

But if illumination neglects serenity, then aggressiveness appears.[25]

When illumination neglects serenity, we fail grief. We see the oneness of all experience, but not the distinctness of each experience. And so we want to skip the uncomfortable, the difficult, the excruciating. We rush grief into the ocean, and we fail to let our tears be realized as the ocean.

But if serenity neglects illumination, murkiness leads to wasted dharma.[26] If we forget the ocean's wideness, the vastness of each moment, we may end up locking onto some experience, holding it, deifying it, making it the point. Then we can't move, we won't move. This is that habit of letting sorrow become an ongoing identity. Our minds and hearts are murky; there's no life, no spark. *When silent illumination is fulfilled, the lotus blossoms, the dreamer awakens/A hundred streams flow into the ocean, a thousand ranges face the highest peak.*[27]

This zazen that is beyond limiting characterization is what is transmitted; it is "the unspoken thing." It doesn't rush and neither does it hold on. If anything, it is "the space in between." It transforms lives of desire and despair into vital expressions of loving wisdom. To practice zazen in this way is not easy, and it has dimensions and depth to it that we can spend lifetimes just beginning to appreciate. Hongzhi says: *Our school's affair hits the mark straight and true. Transmit it to all directions without desiring to gain credit.*[28] Why? Because buildings keep falling. Everyone we love is falling, this body that loves is falling. Desire to stop the sorrow will arise ceaselessly. And there is no interest here in selling anything to you. Turn to what is real. Live what is true. That is all.

Memorial Poem for September Eleventh

Thousands of blossoms
red, brown, white, yellow, black
scattered on ground
made tender by their falling.
This human body, more fragile
than the dew drops
on the countless tips
of morning grass.

Aiiyyee.....

My wailing voice
is the bright September wind
and in the dark night silence speaks:
I will die only when love dies
and you will not let love die.

Uninterrupted Radiance

Yunmen's Sidetrack: Case 39

The Main Case:
A monk said to Yunmen, "The radiance serenely illuminates the whole vast universe...."
Before he had finished the line, Yunmen interrupted him, asking: "Aren't those the words of Zhangzhuo?"
The monk replied, "Yes, they are."
Yunmen said, "You have misspoken."
Later, Master Sixin asked, "Tell me, where did the monk misspeak?"

Wumen's Commentary:
If you can see the uncompromising and rigorous operation of Yunmen's method, and how the monk misspoke, then you qualify as a teacher of people and devas. If it's not yet clear, then you can't save even yourself.

The Capping Verse:
A line is cast in the waters;

the greedy will be caught.
If your mouth opens just a little bit,
your life is completely lost.[29]

Every teacher, one hopes, has something going for them that is all their own. Since every life teaches, it's imperative for each of us to find our way and offer it generously.

In this koan, we meet Yunmen, who was one of the most influential Zen teachers during China's Tang period, and a major player in East Asian Buddhism. Let's first look at what might give a spark like that to a way of teaching.

Zhaozhu's way was described as "light dripping from the lips." Every time he spoke, truth seemed to simply radiate. Like one of those great mother-energy types, he was said to be such a welcoming spirit that no one could be in his presence without being subtly illuminated. Deshan, on the other hand, "carried a big stick"—there was no way to win with him, to get it right; however you responded, you'd be hit. You were in the trap of "this" and "that," whatever you said. And if you went quiet, he'd still drag you out for a "beating." All that was left was to be searingly real. In that absolute bareness, his students found their life.

With Yunmen, what was special was the intoxicating freedom he offered, and his incredible flexibility. He never seemed to be tied down or limited—by context, by form, by language, by anything. Wherever the student was coming from, Yunmen was immediately right there, with an agility that is stunning as one studies his teachings. His ability to cut off whatever his student was preoccupied with—and to follow up with a meeting of acute appropriateness—is, to my mind, unparalleled.

Every teacher is charged with meeting in the heart, meeting

without sticking, meeting without any preconceived device. Perhaps this is the charge, in essence, of every human life. But the mastery within the lineage of that charge, if you will, is demonstrated nowhere more vibrantly than in the "style-less" style of Yunmen. I've often found that his koans bring on a deep, quiet sense of humility, even as there is that quickening we're familiar with when something of beauty is happening. To see him so sharp and alive, one can't help but see in oneself the places of dullness, where that voice we all know so well makes us hesitate: "Not yet, not yet." Yunmen represents, at least for me, the dynamic call of a fully met life, taken up dynamically, with real freshness in the heart-to-heart play of self and other, with each moment a fire in the *hara*.

As we look into today's koan with Yunmen, and into this issue of Zhangzhuo's words—and by inference, into the nature of true voice, authenticity, and autonomy—we'll need to explore how that call to freshness is made. We'll need to look at how it awakens in our lives, and how it works within a tradition that by its very existence as "tradition" might seem intrinsically to contradict freshness. Yunmen and Dogen can no more avoid this undercurrent beneath the surface of their overt dialogues than any of us can. Where will we find ourselves amid the flow of teachings, of culture, family and history—of quotations, references and traditions? How can we free ourselves, as the modern scholar has asked, of the "anxiety of influence"?

Dogen once described what a "right" teacher is—the kind of teacher who has that freshness and fire: "A right teacher is one who…gives no precedence to words and letters, nor to intellectual understanding. With an unusual understanding and extraordinary will-power, he or she neither clings to selfishness, nor indulges in sentimentality. She or he is the individual in whom living and understanding correspond to each other."[30]

Hee-Jin Kim comments on this vibrant passage in *Dogen Kigen, Mystical Realist*, and in doing so, opens up the implicit stream of questions that underlie it: "More often than not, Dogen exalted and adored his teacher with tears of gratitude and joy, so much so that we're given the impression of rhetoric getting the upper hand of factual description. What is most significant was his absolute devotion to the person he considered to be the right teacher, and consequently to the authority and tradition that the teacher represented. Such was the case in spite of his equally indomitable defiance of power and authority—and furthermore, in spite of his respect for intellectual independence."[31]

As we take up this matter personally, many things can be stirred. Kim's reference to Dogen's gratitude, joy, and dedication points to undeniably pleasurable states of consciousness, states that are associated with confidence or certainty. To encounter even the reference can stimulate a yearning to feel likewise, or a memory of having felt like that. His words may even vibrate along with similar feelings we currently have about a tradition, teacher, or authority. We may want there to be someone or something that has a bigger, better, or less vulnerable perspective than our own, or we might remember fondly a time when we believed that there was such a person or thing. Then again, his words may bring to renewed awareness our confidence in our teachers or the teaching.

But there is inevitably some level of tension, that childlike yearning for a parental presence—whether it be God, or an enlightened master—bucking up against a sense of absolute responsibility and intuitive capability. This tension, which is the basic tension of spiritual practice, is where the koan enters. It is the tension of knowing that we're home, yet paradoxically being aware that we have such a long way to go to get there.

Yunmen interrupts the monk, breaks the flow of his intention. This is the place where we feel the prick of the koan, where we know its emotional reality. We can sense what just happened. This young, unnamed monk arrives in front of the teacher. He's got a poem on his tongue, a famous one. He's going to use it to set up his question, to face the teacher—and through that facing, to face himself.

We've all done this—carried our well-crafted whatever to the heart-to-heart meeting—which then, of course, surprises us by having a life far greater than our craft. We do it in formal Zen training situations, and we do it with all sorts of other relationships and situations. We believe that we can imagine it all ahead of time, like directors in a drama where we play all the parts—moving people around like puppets on our stage, figuring out what we'll say, what they'll say.

This monk begins reciting a lay student's—Zhangzhuo's—enlightenment poem:

> The radiance serenely illumines the whole universe;
> the ignorant, the wise, all beings are in my abode.
> When no thought rises, the whole is revealed;
> if the six sense organs move even a little, it is obscured by clouds.
> If you cut off your ignorance, your ailment will increase;
> if you look for the truth, you are wrong.
> Living in accord with things of the world you have no obstructions.
> Nirvana and life-and-death are like colors in a dream.[32]

The turning place, the bone of this poem, is obviously in the lines, "If you cut off your ignorance, your ailment will increase. If you look for the truth, you're wrong." Zhangzhuo is bringing it to that place of *wu wei*—profound non-doing. No cutting off of ignorance, no correcting reality, no seeking after truth, no going somewhere else. He's pointing to the genuine realization of Ango, of peaceful dwelling. No contrivance. No craft. Or, to use the language of another tradition, he's pointing to the realization of Sabbath, about which Abraham Heschel wrote so beautifully: "Labor is a craft, but perfect rest is an art.…How else express glory in the presence of eternity, if not by the silence of abstaining from noisy acts? These restrictions utter songs to those who know how to stay at a palace with a queen."[33] How many, I wonder, will know, really know, the song uttered by the restriction "Just sit still. Just sit still." So, this monk with Zhangzhuo's "Sabbath" poised on his tongue is perhaps on his way to a question.

If Yunmen had waited for the question, we can assume that the dialogue would have been altogether different. But he didn't wait. He interrupted. This is not a common thing. Most of the time, in the classic koans at any rate, the teachers actually let the students finish the questions they've begun. You may not have experienced that at Zen Mountain Monastery, but from the records, it looks for all the world like students generally finish their sentences. Even when they're quoting, as in one of my favorite koans from *The Blue Cliff Record*—Case 40, when Nanchuan meets Luxuan:

Luxuan said, *"Dharma Master Sengzhao once said, 'Heaven and earth and I have the same root. The myriad things and I are one.' This poem is quite marvelous."*

Nanchuan then called Luxuan over close to him, and pointing to a flower in the garden, said, *"People these days see this flower as if they were in a dream."*[34]

It seems such a gentle teaching, doesn't it? These two, walking in the garden, poems and flowers and dreams….Still, understand that "people these days" is a polite Chinese way of saying, "You. Right now." So, effectively, Nanchuan has just said, "You are in some kind of dream. I don't want to point any fingers here, but let's be straight. You're blabbering on and on, while not seeing what's right under your nose." This is thunderous, cutting love.

But here, with Yunmen and our nameless monk, we have this wonderful rip in the journey. The monk is heading in one direction. Yunmen rips the fabric, tears it apart, and takes it another direction from the one the monk thought they would go.

Whatever point the monk thought he was about to make… forget about it.

"Aren't those the words of Zhangzhuo?" And so we have the interruption, the fact of it to reckon with. What is it, really, to be interrupted? The koan is that state of mind. Our idea—direction, intention, agenda—is functioning. Suddenly, the unanticipated and perhaps unwelcome thing arrives and alters the course, the movement, the feeling. We're challenged to realize: what essentially interrupts what? Of course, the spiritually correct solution is obvious to any Zen student. "There is no interruption. Every moment is my path. So, when the 'interruption' arrives, it simply becomes my path, my direction. My practice is the trust in this truth." You can practically feel the white light, the aura of serenity. Can't you?

And of course, it's true. We all know that it's true.

But it's also a little off. Something is missing, and when the koan of interruption is understood with a realization this shallow, what's missing shows in a life. Truth has at least two gates, each of them whole and beautiful, but to hold onto only one makes for a pretty stuck personality. Consider, for a moment, those of you who study the precepts and work with the Renewal of Vows liturgy, why the words "lead the people" appear there. To stop in this koan prematurely is to fail to lead, and there is more to this matter than just being wishy-washy, or just going with the flow. We are not here to follow. Our lives are not fill-in-the-blank tests. This is where the metaphor of "the path" reaches its limit. Nobody has gone here before. But it is true that your way has been interrupted. That may be, in fact, the basic nature of your way. The question remains: now what?

Yesterday, as I was walking through the woods, I came across one of the new deer. There are new beings figuring it out everywhere right now on the mountain. It's that time of year. This little speckled, wobbly thing suddenly came out onto the path I walk each morning, and we squared off, less than a foot or so apart. A voice came from this deer that I don't think any deer has ever used before. I can't even describe it. (And it should never happen again!) It was just a brand new thing.

Immensity taps at our life and finds us—if we allow ourselves to accommodate the interruption. In the Zen tradition, teachers are sometimes employed to do that tapping, to make that interruption—to, in some sense, represent immensity in the student's life and mind, to bring mortality or wonder to the window. But we create teachers and teaching by studying, by letting the dharma grow like redwoods near where we cook, by inviting an interruption of the seeming contraction and smallness of the daily affair: "Where are you?" "How large is this?"

The monk in our koan carries in someone's bald words about a radiance that illuminates uninterruptedly—and is met by interruption. In that moment, he's challenged (as we all are in this and every moment) to show the radiance at work.

Are those someone else's words? Yes. And there the world falls, as it does for each of us. From one of my old journals, a contemplation on confidence, chewing on this same issue of claiming:

"Is this moment, inarguable, firm in its presence, not the heart of life? This is where we have to know the bones of our feet, William Carlos Williams[35] *might say. Where we find ground, and arrive perpetually home. The poem, he did say, is a 'structure built upon your own ground…your ground where you stand on your own feet.'"*

To be that poem is the bone chewed, today, every day. Its hardness meets the hardness of teeth: there is only this gnawing at the matter, this meeting of white and white. Every dog knows this is contentment. Reading the beautiful Henry Bugbee in *The Inward Morning*: "Certainty may be quite compatible with being at a loss to say what one is certain of. Indeed I seriously doubt if the notion of 'certainty of,' or 'certainty that' will take us accurately to the heart of the matter."[36] And later, "So far as we are sensitive to the absoluteness of our situation, we live in a dimension of meaning which is the depth of our experience—we live in eternity."[37]

What is it to commit to this dimension that is depth of experience, that is eternity? "*Somos el tiempo, el río indivisible*" (We are time itself, the indivisible river), Borges says in "Elígía de un parque." It is all over-saying, but we so seldom live it with that great gutsy faith in the truth of it, perhaps it must be said. And said with the certainty of bone, that the feet may become themselves, and get dancing.

> Yunmen said, "Aren't those Zhangzhuo's words?"
> The monk said, "Yes."
> Yunmen said, "You have misspoken."

What is it to "misspeak"? The implication here is that there is something else that is true speech, or perhaps a silence that is truer than anything we can say. Is there a word that is essential, and called for right now? Or is it that the moment you start speaking, you're already adding something extra? If that were true, it would be true of every koan, every talk, every sutra, and every "I love you." Everything said, everything ever created—all nothing but "misspeaking."

But surely silence isn't sufficient to the matter, right? Some would say that this monk misspoke because he answered in the affirmative, falling into duality. "Yes" and "no" seem an obvious error. "Yes" failed to claim the poem. "No" would have been a kind of theft—a tacit plagiarism. They were, after all, Zhang-zhuo's words. It would be creepy to deny that.

But if the monk's error was not simply that he quoted—because what, indeed, is not in some sense a reference to what has already happened—and neither "yes" nor "no" would save him, what might? What is a fresh and free response? Where is the radiance that is uninterrupted?

This is what the commentary calls Yunmen's "rigorous uncompromising method." There is no escaping the demand. It is not relevant only to some other time or situation. It interrupts our agenda completely. What is it demanding? Where is the true voice of this monk? To work on this in formal koan study is to put yourself in his place, and deal with it. What comes up? Don't you want to have the right answer? Most students will usually want so badly to just get it right. We come into that *dokusan* room for face-to-face teaching, we're working with this koan, and we'd like—to be honest—to somehow get on to the next one. Yes, we'd like the spiritual transformation, but we also don't enjoy being stuck on the same koan for years, facing our own dullness. Others have presented something that the teacher recognized. There must be a way to get it right.

"He's put the line in the water," the poem says. "The greedy will be caught." We try to get something, to have something, to know something. Get on that line, get in the cage: there's our life. What is the hook on Yunmen's line? How does it work? It's not so hard to recognize. One day, it's the voice that says, "I'll say it right, do it right. Work diligently, practice hard, and get myself all corrected." Another day, it's the voice that says, "I'll do nothing. You're supposed to do nothing, right? I'm not supposed to cut off my ignorance, so I'll just be really ignorant. I'm not supposed to look for truth? Okay, fine. I don't know."

Yunmen interrupts both voices, and asks for what's real—for genuine, gut-driven aliveness. He cuts—like death cuts into a day—through the greedy, let-me-just-get-it mind we bring to the dialogue, and holds us in depth, in immense and mysterious love. May we let his teaching keep our "mouths from opening," as the poem says, seeking one something after another, babbling on about things.

And may we misspeak, without all this hesitancy about the constancy of our error, in accord with the natural courage with which intimacy interrupts all things. That, after all, is Yunmen's example, and the call that he leaves in the air, vibrating. "Radiance illuminates the whole universe." Say, whose words are those?

Untitled

nothing but
red maple
when
red maple
is

Ma-tsu's White and Black

Book of Equanimity, Case 6

A Stage Whisper:
Where you can't open your mouth, a tongueless person
can speak; where you lift your feet without rising, a legless
person can walk. If you fall within their range and die
at the phrase, how can you have any freedom? When the
four mountains all oppress you, how can you penetrate
to freedom?

Main Case:
A monastic asked Great Master Ma-tsu, "Apart from the
four propositions and beyond the hundred negations,
please directly point out the meaning of living Buddhism."
Ma-tsu said, "I'm tired today and can't explain for you. Go
ask Zhizhang."
The monastic asked Zhizhang; Zhizhang said, "Why don't
you ask the teacher?"
The monastic said, "The teacher told me to come ask you."
Zhizhang said, "I have a headache today and can't explain

for you. Ask Brother Hai."
The monastic asked Hai, who said, "When I come this far, after all I don't understand."
The monastic related all this back to Ma-tsu. Ma-tsu said, "Zang's head is white, Hai's head is black."

A Verse:
Medicine working as illness—
It is mirrored in the past sages.
Illness working as medicine—
Sure, but who is it?
White head, black head—capable heirs of the house.
Statement or no statement—the ability to cut off the flow.
Clearly sitting, cutting off the road of speech and explanation,
Laughable is the old ancient awl at Vaisali. [38]

This is one of the "Nanto" koans, a variety of koan that is traditionally classified as difficult to pass through. Nanto koans demand a raw and wide presentation, and will be alive with a student for a student's whole life, never settling into the comfort zone. This koan of Ma-tsu deals with the issue of existence itself. It takes up the basic matter of life and death—not just our physical death in the future—but also that undermining and ongoing sense of our present insubstantiality, the sense one can have of not being able to quite grasp a continuous self. It sends us looking for our life, bouncing off our ideas and formulations, right along with this earnest monk.

Recognizing the emptiness of the human condition, Zen is a practical process to "resolve the absence," with a built-in imperative not to be seduced into secondary or superficial projects. We're all familiar, killingly familiar, with the projects that temporarily allay our anxiety but fail to address, much less adequately or ultimately relieve, the underlying existential crisis that eventually drives many to religious practice. The process of engaging the practice could be considered an allegiance to this great matter, rather than sliding off into despair. To travel the heart of the koan with this monk, we have to take that first step into practice, into allowing that we care about the living of this life, and will live that caring completely. For the monk, the first step was to ask.

The four propositions he refers to are a standard Buddhist analysis of the possibilities of the nature of reality. The first proposition is existence. The second is nonexistence. The third is both, and the fourth is neither. The hundred negations are the various ways that you can take up each of those possibilities and turn, negate, obviate, and transform it. A sutra says, "Existence is slandered by exaggeration. Nonexistence is slandered by underestimation. Both existence and nonexistence is slandered by contradiction. Neither existence nor nonexistence is slandered by intellectual fabrication. If you abandon these four propositions, the hundred negations are spontaneously wiped out."[39]

Huang Po said, "If you want to understand directly and immediately, everything is not it. If you say you understand clearly and thoroughly, nothing is not it. Looking at it the other way around, without abandoning the four propositions or the hundred negations, where is the meaning of living Buddhism not clear?"[40]

So, is everything, everywhere "it"? But if we understand "everything everywhere" the ideas become a form of idolatry that flattens the heart. If we say "nothing, no way, nowhere," the apathy that follows the idea also flattens the heart. We're still left with "What is the living meaning of an awakened life?" Is there a life that is clear, that's not deluded, that's not simply a series of compromises and crises? If that life is possible, does that mean there is an independent self, or not?

David Loy, Buddhist scholar and social critic, asks:

> How shall we understand anatta "nonself," that strange Buddhist teaching which denies the self we take for granted in our everyday lives? … Today we must relate the anatta doctrine to what we know (or think we know) about the self and the way that self relates to its world.… We can use the psychoanalytic understanding of repression to help us understand anatta, and vice-versa. Then anatta implies that our primary repression is not sexual wishes (as Freud thought), nor even death fears (as many existential psychologists think) but awareness of nonself—the intuition that "I am not real"—which we become conscious of … as a sense of lack infecting our empty (sunya) core. Buddhism analyzes the sense of self into sets of impersonal psycho-physical phenomena whose interaction creates the illusion of self-consciousness—that consciousness is the attribute of the self. The death-repression emphasized by existential psychology transforms the Oedipal complex into what Norman Brown calls an Oedipal project: the attempt to become the father of oneself, i.e., one's own origin.… Buddhism merely shifts the emphasis: the Oedipal project is the attempt of the developing sense of self to attain autonomy, the quest to deny one's groundlessness by becoming one's own ground.[41]

We can see how subtle issues of confidence and self-trust

are within a tradition that recognizes anatta. Trusting oneself involves much more than trusting one's pathology. So what is it? Loy again: "Self-consciousness is not something 'self-existing' but a mental construct, and more like the surface of the sea: dependent on unknown depths that it cannot grasp because it is a manifestation of them."[42]

A friend and I were talking as we walked on the beach, stopping now and then to stare dumbly out at the water. The light was riding around like diamonds on the low waves. I remembered this image and blurted out, "There's a teaching in Buddhism that our consciousness is like the surface of the sea." She surprised me with this exuberant response, "That's right! Why do we think the things we do? Why do I think what I think and you think what you think? Suddenly I'll be thinking about pineapples!"

Consciousness is trying to grasp oneself by virtue of the surface of the sea. The problem arises when this conditioned consciousness wants to ground itself—to make itself real. If the sense of self is an always insecure construct, its efforts to realize itself will be attempts to objectify itself in some fashion. The ego self is this never-ending project to objectify oneself. [43]

The endlessness of the project is also important to taste: when the teaching points to ceaseless practice, it is a response to and liberation of this never-ending project to objectify oneself. Our *dukkha* (suffering or anxiety) projects, the projects of the dissatisfied mind, whether they're laudable or laughable, all fail. This seems a major part of the challenge of maturity: we recognize that whether we're being good, being successful, being powerful, whether we're having stuff or love or pleasure, whether we're doing right or doing nothing, all of it is shadowed by this ultimate lack of ultimacy. It is easy as we get older and the disappointments mount up to climb into a pit of sadness, or to just lose touch with how to generate any energy to begin anything with trust.

The consequence of the perpetual failure (of the ego to reify itself) is that the sense of self has, as its inescapable shadow, a sense of lack, which it always tries to escape….We experience this deep sense of lack as the persistent feeling that "there is something wrong with me…The problem with our objectifications is that no object can ever satisfy if it's not really an object we want.[44]

My brother collects lighters. My friend is a team person; she loves Florida State University. Maybe we collect silence, treasure the dharma, trust trees. Regardless of the object, though, whether it's material abundance or spiritual ideologies, to the extent that it's objectified, it will fail us. The bottom will drop out. This is why it becomes so compelling to clarify what's going on—that failing hurts so much. Democracy will fail, Zen will fail. Love won't work, and the enlightened examples won't do either. The breadth of the failure is utterly scathing. Over and over again we get the idea going, and then feel it short-sheet us. Whether the pain is sharp or deep or just annoying, we're apt to feel betrayed by the way it keeps happening, constantly conspiring toward collapse.

When we don't understand what is actually motivating us— because what we think we want is only a symptom of something else (our desire to become real, which is essentially a spiritual yearn- ing)—we end up compulsive….Any truly satisfactory resolution of this situation must address the root problem, my lack of self. This can lead to an awakening that transforms my lack from such a festering anxiety into a 'empty' source of creativity. The self's sense of separa-

tion from the world motivates me to try to secure myself within it, but the only authentic solution is the essentially spiritual realization that I am not other than it.[45]

The monastic asks, *"Apart from the four propositions and the hundred negations, please point out to me directly the meaning of living Buddhism."* Wansong comments on this, *"Everywhere they call this a question in the mouth of a shackle; but Ma-tsu wasn't flustered—he just said, 'I'm too tired to tell you today. Go ask Zhizhang.' He spared his own eyebrows and pierced that monastic's nose."*

When Buddhist teachers explain too much it's said that their eyebrows fall out. When a student's nose is pierced, it's like when a small ring is placed in the nose of a large ox, enabling a farmer to move it around with ease. Here, with few words and no explanation, Ma-tsu moves the monastic away from his expected path. "I'm too tired" is not what a teacher is "supposed" to be or say; what creates a teacher is the fact of teaching. Is this teaching, or excusing himself? That lumbering ox may be led around by whatever idea forms right at this point. This is where it's so important to pay attention to what we project, what we assume is happening when we don't get the response we anticipate: whether the koan is from the formal collections, or from daily life.

Zhizhang, too, "fit in the groove without contrivance" when he responded to the monastic, *"Why don't you ask the teacher?"* The monastic still didn't open his eyes; he said, *"The teacher told me to come to you."* Zhizhang said, *"I've got a headache today. I can't explain for you. Go ask Brother Hai."* The monastic asked Hai, who said, *"When I come this far, after all I don't understand."*

Wansong's comment on this is telling: *"I thought it was Houbai (the thief), but here is even Houhei (who robbed Houbai by trickery)."* In other words, Hai steals the illusion from this monastic, but the monastic thinks nothing has happened. He doesn't even know the thief is in the house. There's this incredible compassionate activity meeting this monastic at his every turn, and still he is unable to recognize it, much less feel and be moved by it. Sound familiar? So much of spiritual practice involves waking up to some ongoing kindness or rightness that we've somehow ignored for days or even years, and then practicing the regret at what we feel we've kind of wasted, letting the humility of that transform into vow. This can be really hard when we realize that others around us got it right away, or much earlier, while we bumbled on with our self-absorption blinding us. This monastic doesn't have that challenge yet; he's still got the blinders on securely.

He completes the circle by returning to Ma-tsu, and recounting his journey. Ma-tsu responds, *"Zang's head is white, Hai's head is black."* The comment says, *"This statement kills everyone in the world with doubt."* There's a surface interpretation of this that we can look at first, just to get it out of the way. Zang, in saying *"I have a headache,"* takes up a thing—the headache—revealing the whole thing through one thing. Therefore, his head is white. Hai, who says, *"When I come this far, after all I don't understand,"* takes up nothing, not knowing, non-separation, the absolute. His head is black, where no distinctions can be discerned. However, with this kind of analysis we are still left with the resounding "So what?" How does this speak to the issue at all? The hundred negations and four propositions gone, wordless, we face this life directly.

Wansong helps open this up: *"I say 'four in the morning, three at night'—they are glad or mad without reason."* Explanations don't reach this point. The neat aligning of "Ah, that's an answer from the absolute; that's an answer from the relative" doesn't get to the heart of the matter. About *"Zang's head is white, Hai's head is black,"* he says "*a duck's head is green, a crane's head is red,*" blowing the color-scheme metaphor on absolute and relative out of the water entirely.

What is the reality of living Buddhism? "The ten-shadowed spiritual horse stands south of the ocean, the five-colored auspicious unicorn walks north of the sky. People everywhere, don't depend on a fox spirit."[46] This is a repeat of the advice we can't seem to hear often enough: don't let it become tricky. Don't think it's something contrived that you have to figure out, look up in the back of the book: what does white mean? What is really being revealed here? A Zen koan is not something to memorize and have in your pocket as a reference.

Ernest Becker in *The Birth and Death of Meaning* expresses much the same point using some interesting language:

Idolatry occurs whenever we try to become real by completely identifying with something in the world as the source of our power. The problem of life is how to grow out of our idolatries: Human beings believe either in God or in idols. There is no third course open, for God is the only object who is not a concrete object. God is abstract necessity, the unconditioned, and this is liberating rather than opposing or confining, even though we submit our energies to it. Humanity achieves its highest freedom when its energies are allied with the unconditioned cosmic process.[47]

Ma-tsu's koan takes up the implications for basic self-trust within groundlessness. For many American Buddhists it seems that the moment God enters the sentence, a kind of shut-down occurs. "I don't believe in that. Been there; done that. It didn't work. Don't like it. It scares me. It's going to get stupid." We just stop hearing in a deep way. Loy comments, "The touchstone of authentic spirituality is not whether one believes in God but whether one believes in and works to ground one's energies in what Becker calls the unconditioned cosmic process." Grounding the mystery of being in one's own life is practicing one's own life. It's an ineffable trust that can thoroughly change how we live and love this life.

"Zang's head is white, Hai's head is black." There's a footnote to this line that says, *"Investigate for thirty more years."* It's not accomplished in a weekend, or even in a thousand centuries. When is it finished? When does it begin? An old friend once changed my sense of what's possible just by saying "I'll never finish loving you." To discern this life, we need to practice this life. Is this apart from the world? Is this the world itself? Is it neither? Is it both?

Putting aside all that, who will realize the living meaning of an awakened life?

Mill Poem

My old eyes preferred
The hundreds of white flowers
To these lost golf balls

Notes

(Endnotes)

1 Diogenes Allen, *Temptation (New York: Seabury Books, 2004), 54.*

2 Robert Aitken, *The Gateless Barrier: The Wu-Men Kuan of Mumonkan (New York: North Point Press, 1990), 152.*

3 John Daido Loori, *The True Dharma Eye: Zen Master Dōgen's Three Hundred Kōans (Boston: Shambhala Publications, 2005), 34.*

4 Nyogen Senzaki and Ruth Strout McCandless, *The Iron Flute: 100 Zen Kōan, with commentary by Genrō, Fugai and Nyogen (Tokyo: C.E. Tuttle, 1961), 111.*

5 Ibid.

6 Adapted from Mumon Ekai, *The Gateless Gate, translated by Nyogen Senzaki and Paul Reps (Los Angeles: J. Murray, 1934), koan 8.*

7 Aitken, *The Gateless Barrier, 61.*

8 Ibid., 62-3.

9 George C. Williams, *The Pony Fish's Glow: And Other Clues to Plan and Purpose in Nature* (New York: Basic Books, 1997), 158.

10 Francis H. Cook, *Sounds of Valley Streams: Enlightenment in Dōgen's Zen, translation of nine essays from Shōbōgenzō* (Albany: State University of New York Press, 1989).

11 Ibid.

12 Ibid.

13 Ibid.

14 Ibid.

15 E.L. Doctorow, "Doctorow," *Writers at Work: The Paris Review Interviews, 8th series*, ed. George Plimpton (New York: Viking, 1988), 318.

16 Cook, *Sounds of Valley Streams*.

17 Reiho Masunaga, *A Primer of Sōtō Zen: a translation of Dōgen's Shōbōgenzō zuimonki* (Honolulu: University of Hawaii Press, 1975), 39.

18 Ibid.

19 Ibid.

20 Cook, *Sounds of Valley Streams*.

21 Taigen Daniel Leighton, *Cultivating the Empty Field: The Silent Illumination of Zen Master Hongzhi* (Boston: Tuttle, 2000), 67.

22 Kirsten Bakis, *Lives of the Monster Dogs* (New York: Farrar Straus & Giroux, 1997), 273-4.

23 Ibid., 276.

24 Ibid., 277.

25 Leighton, *Cultivating the Empty Field,* 67.

26 Ibid., 68.

27 Ibid.

28 Ibid.

29 Adapted from Aitken, *The Gateless Barrier,* 235.

30 Hee-Jin Kim, *Dōgen Kigen, Mystical Realist (Tucson: Association for Asian Studies, University of Arizona Press, 1975).*

31 Ibid.

32 Aitken, *The Gateless Barrier,* 236.

33 Abraham J. Heschel, "A Palace in Time," in *The Ten Commandments: The Reciprocity of Faithfulness,* ed. William P. Brown *(Louisville: Westminster John Knox Press, 2004), 215.*

34 Adapted from Yuanwu, Thomas F. Cleary, and J. C. Cleary, *The Blue Cliff Record (Boulder, CO: Shambhala, 1977).*

35 William Carlos Williams, *The Autobiography of William Carlos Williams (New York: Random House, 1951), 376.*

36 Henry Greenwood Bugbee, *The Inward Morning: A Philosophical Exploration in Journal Form (Athens, GA: University of Georgia Press, 1999), 36.*

37 Ibid., 37.

38 Adapted from Xingxiu and Thomas Cleary, *Book of Serenity: One Hundred Zen Dialogues (New York: Lindisfame Press, 1990).*

39 Ibid.

40 Adapted from Hsiu Pei, John Blofeld, and Qi Duan, *The Zen Teaching of Huang Po: On the Transmission of Mind (London: Rider & Co., 1958).*

41 David R. Loy, *Buddhist History of the West: Studies in Lack (Albany: State University of New York Press, 2002).*

42 Ibid.

43 David R. Loy, "What Are You Really Afraid Of?" *Tricycle Magazine* 12, no. 4 (Summer 2003). https://tricycle.org/magazine/what-are-you-really-afraid/

44 David R. Loy, "Avoiding the Void: The Lack of Self in Psychotherapy and Buddhism," *Journal of Transpersonal Psychology 24(2) (1992): 151-179.*

45 David R. Loy, "Buddhism and Money: The Repression of Emptiness Today," *Buddhist Ethics and Modern Society 31(1991): 297-312.*

46 Xingxiu and Cleary, *Book of Serenity.*

47 Ernest Becker, *The Birth and Death of Meaning: An Interdisciplinary Perspective on the Problem of Man* (New York: The Free Press, 1962).

Bibliography

Aitken, Robert. *The Gateless Barrier: The Wu-Men Kuan of Mumonkan.* New York: North Point Press, 1990.

Allen, Diogenes. *Temptation.* New York: Seabury Books, 2004.

Bakis, Kirsten. *Lives of the Monster Dogs.* New York: Farrar Straus & Giroux, 1997.

Becker, Ernest. *The Birth and Death of Meaning: An Interdisciplinary Perspective on the Problem of Man.* New York: The Free Press, 1962.

Bugbee, Henry Greenwood. *The Inward Morning: A Philosophical Exploration in Journal Form.* Athens, GA: University of Georgia Press, 1999.

Cleary, Thomas F. and J. C. Cleary, editors. *The Blue Cliff Record (Yuanwu).* Boulder, CO: Shambhala, 1977.

Cleary, Thomas F. and Xiagxiu. *Book of Serenity: One Hundred*

Zen Dialogues. New York: Lindisfame Press, 1990.

Cook, Francis H. *Sounds of Valley Streams: Enlightenment in Dōgen's Zen, translation of nine essays from Shōbōgenzō. Albany: State University of New York Press, 1989.*

Doctorow, E.L. "Doctorow." In *Writers at Work: The Paris Review Interviews, 8th series, edited by George Plimpton. New York: Viking, 1988.*

Heschel, Abraham J. "A Palace in Time." In *The Ten Commandments: The Reciprocity of Faithfulness, edited by William P. Brown. Louisville: Westminster John Knox Press, 2004.*

Kim, Hee-Jin. *Dōgen Kigen, Mystical Realist. Tucson: Association for Asian Studies, University of Arizona Press, 1975.*

Leighton, Taigen Daniel. *Cultivating the Empty Field: The Silent Illumination of Zen Master Hongzhi. Boston: Tuttle, 2000.*

Loori, John Daido. *The True Dharma Eye: Zen Master Dōgen's Three Hundred Kōans. Boston: Shambhala Publications, 2005.*

Loy, David R. "Avoiding the Void: The Lack of Self in Psychotherapy and Buddhism." In *Journal of Transpersonal Psychology 24(2), 1992.*

———. "Buddhism and Money: The Repression of Emptiness Today," In *Buddhist Ethics and Modern Society 31, 1991.*

———.*Buddhist History of the West: Studies in Lack.* Albany: State University of New York Press, 2002.

———. "What Are You Really Afraid Of?" In *Tricycle Magazine* 12, no. 4 (Summer 2003).

Masunaga, Reiho. *A Primer of Sōtō Zen: a translation of Dōgen's Shōbōgenzō zuimonki.* Honolulu: University of Hawaii Press, 1975.

Pei, Hsiu, John Blofeld, and Qi Duan. *The Zen Teaching of Huang Po: On the Transmission of Mind.* London: Rider & Co., 1958.

Senzaki, Nyogen and Ruth Strout McCandless. *The Iron Flute: 100 Zen Kōan, with commentary by Genrō, Fugai and Nyogen.* Tokyo: C.E. Tuttle, 1961.

Senzaki, Nyogen and Paul Reps, translators. *Mumon Ekai: The Gateless Gate.* Los Angeles: J. Murray, 1934.

Williams, George C. *The Pony Fish's Glow: And Other Clues to Plan and Purpose in Nature.* New York: Basic Books, 1997.

Williams, William Carlos. *The Autobiography of William Carlos Williams.* New York: Random House, 1951.

Acknowledgements

On the trail up to the cemetery at Zen Mountain Monastery, there's one tree so wide and tall that from the first time seeing it I called it Grandmother. It was my first walk on the two-hundred-acre property where I would end up living twenty-four years as a Zen monastic, and eventually serving as Vice-Abbot. Where so much else seemed intense, vaguely male, this great and gracious tree, branches bare in the calm woods, let me know I could trust the ground my feet were standing on. She was a reminder and expression of what had brought me to give myself over to the quiet I knew again when I saw her—both perfect and rich with unanswerable questions. So, my first gratitude is to the silence.

In the early years during which the talks in *Empty Branches* were given, helpers were many, and I will no doubt forget to list all names. You were at a retreat and during silent work practice, your assignment was to transcribe dharma talks. One transcriber: Janice Senju Baker, I remember your great care and attention to detail. Angela Mujaku Caponigro, who not only transcribed, but secreted away copies of talks and wrote to me for years with questions and comments: I miss you, dear sister and student. I would never have felt as at ease being published in *Mountain Record*, *Tricycle*, and elsewhere were it not for the initial editing of my talks by the kind and skillful Rod Huntress. The push to gather and collect, look again and organize this work, is the "fault" of the very gifted Alice Peck, without whose encouragement these words—based on talks given over many years—would have never seen the light again. My thanks as well to Ruth Mullen, for her attention to copy editing, and to the deft and artful Duane Stapp, who has elevated the whole affair with his book and cover design.

Made in United States
Orlando, FL
09 May 2022